The Barnyard Bunch

COOL COWS

Ryan James

Norwood House Press

Cataloging-in-Publication Data

Names: James, Ryan.
Title: Cool cows / Ryan James.
Description: Buffalo, NY : Norwood House Press, 2026. | Series: The barnyard bunch | Includes glossary and index.
Identifiers: ISBN 9781978574267 (pbk.) | ISBN 9781978574274 (library bound) | ISBN 9781978574281 (ebook)
Subjects: LCSH: Cows--Juvenile literature. | Livestock--Juvenile literature.
Classification: LCC SF197.5 J359 2026 | DDC 636.2--dc23

Published in 2026 by
Norwood House Press
2544 Clinton Street
Buffalo, NY 14224

Designer: Rhea Magaro
Editor: Kim Thompson

Photo credits: Cover, pp. 1, 10, 18, 21 Clara Bastian/Shutterstock.com; p. 5 Ann Hull/Shutterstock.com; p. 6 Eric Isselee/Shutterstock.com; p. 7 Dany Store/Shutterstock.com; p. 8 Pornsawan Baipakdee/Shutterstock.com; p. 9 Bob Pool/Shutterstock.com; p. 11 Karlie Butler/Shutterstock.com; p. 12 MiQ / Shutterstock.com; p. 14 Joel Masson/Shutterstock.com; p. 1506photo/Shutterstock.com; p. 17 Labellepatine/Shutterstock.com;

Printed in the United States of America

CPSIA compliance information: Batch #CSNHP26: For further information contact Norwood House Press at 1-800-237-9932.

TABLE OF CONTENTS

COOL COWS

Cows are farm animals. They live in the barnyard.

HOW COWS LOOK

Cows come in many colors. Some have spots. No two cows have exactly the same spots.

A cow has a thick **coat**. This helps it stay warm.

Cows have four strong legs. Each leg ends in a **hoof**. Cows are fast runners!

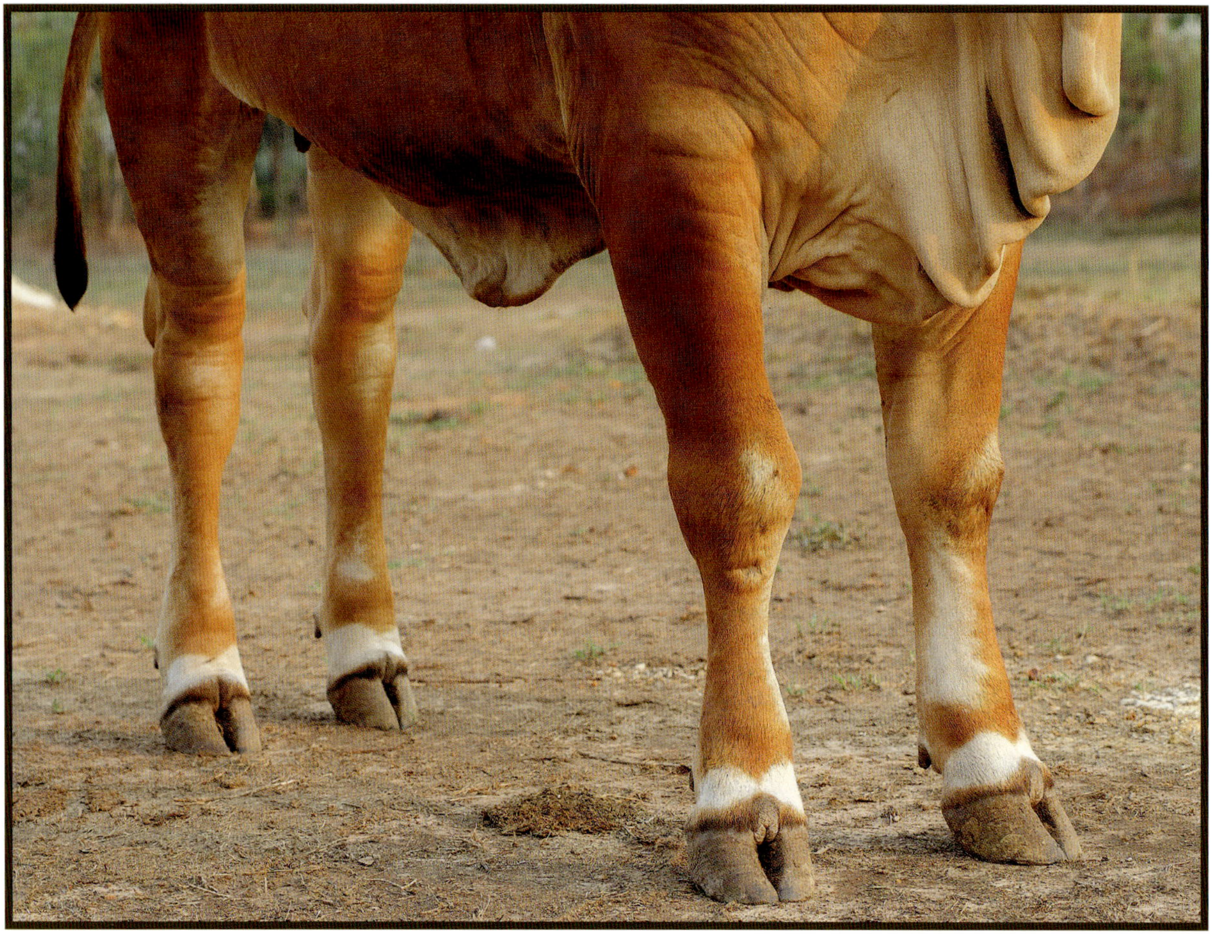

Some cows have **horns**. A cow's horns can grow very long!

HOW COWS SOUND

Cows make different noises to **communicate**. They may grunt when they are hungry.

Cows that feel stressed may **bellow**.

Cows make "moo" sounds. This can send a warning. It can help cows find each other.

WHAT COWS EAT

Cows are **herbivores**. They eat only plants.

When it is warm outside, cows **graze** on grass in **pastures**. When it is cold outside, cows eat **hay**.

Cows eat and drink a lot each day. They can eat 50 pounds (23 kilograms) of food. They can drink 35 gallons (132 liters) of water.

HOW COWS GROW UP

Baby cows are called calves.

Calves drink their mothers' **milk**.

FUN ON THE FARM

Cows like to play and have fun. Cows can even have best friends!

GLOSSARY

bellow (BEL-oh): to make a deep roaring sound

coat (koht): a layer of fur or hair that covers an animal's body

communicate (kuh-MYOO-ni-kate): to share information and feelings

graze (graze): to feed on grass that is growing in a field

hay (hay): long grass that is cut, dried, and used as food for farm animals

herbivores (HUR-buh-vorz): animals that eat only plants

hoof (huf): the hard part that covers a cow's foot

horns (hornz): hard, pointy parts on the top of a cow's head

milk (milk): the white fluid produced by female cows to feed their babies

pastures (PAS-churz): grassy fields where animals graze

THINKING QUESTIONS

1. What are baby cows called?
2. Name three body parts that cows have.
3. What do cows eat?
4. How do cows communicate?
5. What helps a cow run fast?

INDEX

ABOUT THE AUTHOR

Ryan James lives in the mountains of North Carolina, where he goes hiking with his dog Bailey. He loves fly fishing, visiting farms in the area, and picking fresh produce. He has always enjoyed writing and wrote his first book as a teenager.

metamorphosis (met-uh-MOR-fuh-sis): a series of major changes in form and appearance that some animals go through as they become adults; a transformation

molting (MOHL-ting): shedding old skin, feathers, shells, or fur so that new body parts can grow

pupa (PYOO-puh): an insect in an inactive stage of development between a larva and an adult

secretes (si-KREETS): makes and releases a liquid from the body

Thinking Questions

1. Why do you think female butterflies lay eggs on plants?
2. How much can caterpillars grow?
3. What does it mean to molt? Why do caterpillars molt?
4. What happens to a caterpillar inside its chrysalis?
5. What can adult butterflies do?

Index

About the Author

A.B. Clamant is the author of several fact-filled books for kids. The daughter of two grade school teachers, she developed a love of children's books at an early age. When she's not writing, she is working on opening her own petting zoo, ABCs Animals. Her favorite foods are bread, fruit strips, and candy. A.B. Clamant lives in Springfield, Missouri, with her four cats: Monkey, Corky, Prissy, and Nelly.